NOW WHAT?

A GUIDEBOOK FOR NEW CHRISTIANS

RALPH W. HARRIS

GOSPEL PUBLISHING HOUSE
SPRINGFIELD, MISSOURI
02-0558

Congratulations!

I understand you have taken Jesus Christ as your personal Savior. If so, this is the greatest, wisest, best decision you have ever made.

Now what happens? This is just the beginning, you know. This book will help you become a successful, happy Christian.

The next seven days can be the most important week of your life.

You are starting a new life, and this will call for a number of changes. You will need help. The questions I answer in each chapter involve all the areas related to successful Christian living.

You are establishing new patterns. During the next week I will help you do so, if you follow my suggestions.

This is more than a book; it is a plan of action for the next seven days. Each chapter covers one day. I urge you to follow through on every suggestion.

The suggested Bible reading each day will take you through the Gospel of John during this week (it will take less than fifteen minutes a day). This Gospel was written to strengthen the faith of new converts.

The suggested Bible study at the end of each lesson will take very little time, but it will help you learn how to study the Bible. The total time needed each day is less than half an hour. Not much time to ensure having a happy Christian life!

Do your best and God will help you!

1
What Has Happened to Me?

TODAY'S BIBLE READING: John 1, 2, and 3

Just what has happened to you? That's a good question. And an important one. Knowing what happened and what it means will help you the rest of your Christian life.

It happened in a church, in your home, or somewhere else. Someone helped you, or perhaps you were by yourself. But wasn't it something like this? You felt a need, learned somehow that Jesus Christ could help you, and one way or another, asked Him to come into your life.

Now, what does it all mean? Let's put it simply. Two things have happened:

1. Jesus has become your Savior.
2. You have become a child of God.

We call this *salvation*. Perhaps someone has already mentioned that now you are "saved." Maybe you wonder what that means. Saved from what? Why did you need to be saved?

God wants you to know three things:

1. You're a sinner.
2. You cannot save yourself.
3. Only Christ can save you.

The Bible says, "All have sinned" (Romans 3:23). That includes you and me. The Bible also says, "The wages of sin is death" (Romans 6:23). This kind of death is spiritual and eternal.

We cannot save ourselves from this death by our good

works, by church membership, by trying to be good. The only way to be *saved* (there's that word saved) from the penalty is to get rid of our sins.

Now, how can we be saved? Jesus provided a way by dying on the cross. In doing this, He took our place and suffered our punishment. When we ask God to forgive our sins, and believe Jesus died for us, God accepts us for Jesus' sake, our sins are forgiven, and Jesus becomes our Savior.

But something else has happened. *You have become a child of God.*

A child of God? What does that mean? Look at it this way. When you were born as a baby, you received natural life from your parents. Because of this you are like them, you have many of their characteristics.

When Jesus became your Savior, He brought to you new life, spiritual life, life from God. The Bible calls this the new birth (John 3:3). By your first birth you became a child of your earthly parents; by your new, or second, birth you have become a child of God, your Heavenly Father.

This is important! You now have two natures: (1) The old nature you received when born the first time. This we can call the *self-life.* (2) The new nature you received with the second birth. Since Jesus Christ is now living in you by His Holy Spirit, we call this new nature the *Christ-life.*

As far as your first, or natural, birth is concerned, you may be an adult, a youth, or a child. But as far as your new, or spiritual, birth is concerned, you are a baby. You have received a new life, but it's just beginning.

Your spiritual life has to grow. You don't want to remain a spiritual baby; you want to become a mature Christian.

During these next few days I will show you how to grow spiritually. I cannot emphasize too strongly how important these days are. You are establishing the pattern for the rest

4

of your life. You are determining the kind of Christian you will be. If you will follow each suggestion carefully, you will have a happy, successful Christian life.

BIBLE STUDY FOR TODAY (answer in your own words)

John 1:12. What happens to those who receive Christ?
_____

John 1:29. What did John the Baptist call Jesus? _____
_____

John 2:5. What advice did Jesus' mother give to the servants? _____

John 3:3. What is necessary, to "see the kingdom of God"? _____

John 3:6 List the two kinds of birth:

a. _____

b. _____

John 3:16. How can we keep from perishing? _____
_____

John 3:36. What does a person have, if he believes on Jesus? _____
_____

GOOD VERSES TO MEMORIZE: John 1:12; 1:29 (last part); 3:3; 3:16; 3:36

5

2
Where Do I Go from Here?

TODAY'S BIBLE READING: John 4, 5, and 6

On the last page of chapter 1 I told you that you're a spiritual baby and that you need to grow. Where do you go from here? I could have asked, "Where do you *grow* from here?" You see, you're a child of God all right, but you're a baby. You need to grow up spiritually.

Isn't it tragic when, because of a physical affliction, a child fails to mature and mentally remains a baby all his life? Actually, it's even more tragic when a person becomes a child of God through salvation and then fails to grow up spiritually.

This doesn't have to happen to you. If you will follow these suggestions, you can quickly become a strong, mature Christian.

First of all, remember that your spiritual life comes from Jesus Christ, the Son of God. "He that hath the Son hath life" (1 John 5:12). (This is the *Epistle* of John toward the end of the Bible, not the *Gospel* of John.) The preceding verse says, "God has given to us eternal life, and this life is in His Son."

Christ lives in you. Don't forget it.

Receiving life is not enough; you must feed that life. When a baby is born in the natural, it will die unless its parents take care of it. They must feed it and nourish its physical life so it will grow.

This is also true in relation to your new spiritual life. If you feed it, it will grow; if you neglect it, it will die.

It's as simple as that. It depends on you. Now, what will cause you to grow spiritually?

THE BIBLE

Tomorrow we'll talk more about the Bible. Your use or neglect of the Bible will determine the kind of Christian you will be. This is why we're suggesting that you read three chapters each day this week. Get in the habit of reading the Bible every day. "As newborn babes, desire the sincere milk of the word, that ye may grow thereby" (1 Peter 2:2).

PRAYER

In chapter 4 we'll talk about the various kinds of prayer and how to pray effectively. The simplest way to describe prayer is that it is talking to God and letting Him talk to us. Make time every day to pray. The best time is the first thing in the morning, before you get involved with other activities. Talk to Him as you would to a friend—for He is your best Friend. Don't worry about using the right words. God is more concerned with your attitude than with your vocabulary.

WITNESSING

Tell others about what has happened to you. A witness is someone who testifies about something he has learned for himself. If you have learned that Jesus satisfies, let others know about it too.

Witnessing is inviting people to get acquainted with Jesus. Let them know how wonderful your new Friend can be to them. Witnessing will make you a stronger Christian.

REGULAR CHURCH ATTENDANCE

If you take a live coal from the fireplace and put it by

7

itself, it will soon go out. In the same way, Christians need the encouragement of other Christians. Hearing the Word of God, praying with others, singing together, making Christian friendships—these will help you to grow.

OBEDIENCE

When God asks you to do or not to do something, obey quickly. Jesus is your Master as well as your Savior. A good rule for deciding what is right or wrong is: Will this be pleasing to God? Make this the ruling factor in all you do or say.

I'm glad to tell you that spiritual maturity does not depend on how long you have been saved. If you will follow these simple steps, you will become a mature Christian, one of whom God is proud, one He can use.

BIBLE STUDY FOR TODAY

John 4:10. What did Jesus offer to give this woman?

_____

John 4:14. What will be the result if a person drinks of the water Jesus gives? _____

_____

John 4:24. How are we to worship God? _____

_____

John 5:39. What advice about the Bible did Jesus give?

_____

John 6:35. What did Jesus call himself? _____

_____

GOOD VERSES TO MEMORIZE: JOHN 4:14; 5:14 (beginning with "Behold"); 5:24; 6:37

8

3
How Can I Understand the Bible?

TODAY'S BIBLE READING: John 7, 8, and 9

As I told you in chapter 2, the Bible is one of the best ways by which a person can grow spiritually. There are five ways by which the Bible can become a part of your life.

HEARING THE WORD

Notice that I often refer to the Bible as "The Word." This is because it is God's way of communicating with us. We use our words to express ourselves to others; God uses the Bible to express himself to us.

Because hearing is one way of receiving the Word of God into our lives, in these first days and weeks of your Christian experience form the habit of attending every church service possible. There you will hear the Word of God.

Form the habit, too, of sitting near the front of the church, so you will not be distracted. Always take your Bible and look up the passages the speaker refers to. Take notes; it will help you remember helpful points.

READING THE WORD

Another way to get the Word of God into your life is to read it regularly. The kind of habits we form determine our character, and one of the best habits you can form is to read the Bible every day.

Set a reasonable pace for yourself. Start by reading fifteen minutes in the morning and perhaps the same amount before going to bed at night. Carry a New Testament and read it during lunchtime.

For your devotional reading, use a Bible in which you can underline with a pen and perhaps write notes in the margin. See page 24 for suggestions about where to read after you have read the Gospel of John this first time.

STUDYING THE WORD

Deeper study will take more time, but it has more value too. A little later in this chapter you will find helps on this. For studying you will need a longer period, an hour at least—perhaps some evening you have free.

MEMORIZING THE WORD

Notice that each of these gets a little harder. But memorization is one way of obeying the verse, "Thy word have I hid in mine heart" (Psalm 119:11).

Start with some of the verses I am listing each day. First look at the various parts, noticing what each really means. This is very important. Then notice the important words. For example, in Psalm 119:11 the important words are "word," "hid," and "heard." Memorize the reference too.

MEDITATING ON THE WORD

If you have heard, and read, and studied, and memorized the Bible, you have something to meditate on. In the many spare moments during the day—working around the house, waiting for an elevator, driving down the street—you can put your mind in gear. If you can't sleep at night, try thinking about a passage or verse from the Bible.

10

UNDERSTANDING THE BIBLE

There's nothing mysterious about the Bible. Just think of it as God's way of talking to you. However, this outline will help you understand any part of the Bible, long or short.

Points. What does this passage or verse say? What are the various parts? What are the subjects it speaks of?

Problems. What does this verse or passage say that you don't understand? Write down the problems and find the answers later, by your study or by asking an older Christian.

Parallels. What similar thoughts are found elsewhere in the Bible? The more you study, the more help you will have here.

Promises. What blessings and helps are stated or implied?

Perils. What warnings do you find?

Precepts. What commands are stated or implied, for you to obey?

BIBLE STUDY FOR TODAY

John 7:17. What attitude will help a person to know if certain teachings are true? _____

_____

John 7:37–39. What happens to the one who believes on Jesus? _____

_____

John 8:31. How can we really be Jesus' disciples? _____

_____

John 8:32. What will the truth do for people? _____

_____

GOOD VERSES TO MEMORIZE: John 7:37; 8:12; 8:32

4
How Can I Pray Effectively?

TODAY'S BIBLE READING: John 10, 11, and 12

If the Bible can be likened to food, because it nourishes our spiritual lives, then prayer can be likened to our breathing. There are two parts to breathing—breathing in and breathing out. So it is with prayer—the outreach after God, and His response to us.

The person who said, "I can't find time for prayer," was correct. You must *make* time for it. A good way is to do it along with your Bible reading. In fact, I know some people who read their Bibles on their knees; then if some truth grips their hearts, they stop for a few moments and pray about it.

You'll never become a solid, mature Christian without a consistent prayer life.

WHAT TO PRAY ABOUT

What to pray about is one of the first problems you'll meet. You think of your family, your friends, your associates, your own needs—and in five minutes you've run out of subject matter. One way to solve this problem is to channel your prayer into certain directions, a different direction each day. On the inside of the back cover of this booklet are suggestions for doing this.

KINDS OF PRAYER

Another solution to the problem of what to pray about is

to recognize that there are several kinds of prayer. Basically, it is simply talking to God.

Petition. This means asking God to meet certain needs. Though some people never progress beyond the "gimme" stage, always asking God for something, there is nothing wrong with asking the Lord for His help. In fact, He encourages us to come with our needs.

Thanksgiving. Remember, prayer is a two-way street. Don't forget to thank God for what He as already done for you. In fact, this is a good way to begin your prayer times. For one thing, it builds your faith to remember what God has already done for you.

Praise. This is something like thanksgiving but deals with what God *is* instead of what He has *done.* Sometimes you can use one of the Psalms, reading it aloud to express how you feel.

Worship is very close to praise, but is almost an attitude. There will be times when words cannot fully express your feelings, and you can only say praise words like "glory" or "hallelujah." You may even become silent as you kneel or sit, overwhelmed at the sense of how great God is.

Intercession. You may become gripped with the need of someone else, and feel burdened to keep on praying until you have the assurance that God has answered your prayer. This is one of the greatest kinds of prayer, for in it you are thinking of others. We need more of this kind of prayer.

How God Answers

This is an important lesson to learn: God answers every prayer. Sometimes He says, "Yes," sometimes He says, "No," and often He says, "Wait." But time spent in prayer is never wasted. You see, even more than what He does for

13

you, God is interested in what He can do in you. Prayer changes things—and people.

PRAYING IN PUBLIC

Sooner or later, someone will call on you to lead in prayer. Don't get panicky. Simply remember that you're praying to the Lord, not to the people. Pray as a representative of the group and express what you feel are their general desires in that meeting. Don't worry about using exactly the right words.

BIBLE STUDY FOR TODAY

John 10:11. Who is the good shepherd? _____

_____

John 10:15. What has Jesus done for the sheep? _____

_____

John 11:27. Who did Martha say Jesus is? _____

_____

John 11:40. What is needed in order to see God's glory?

_____

John 11:42. How often did the Father hear Jesus' prayer?

_____

John 12:32. What did Jesus mean by "lifted up"? _____

_____

GOOD VERSES TO MEMORIZE: John 10:9; 10:10; 11:25,26; 11:40; 12:25; 12:32

5
How Can I Be a Strong Christian?

TODAY'S BIBLE READING: John 13, 14, and 15

As a Christian, you need strength for two reasons: (1) to live an overcoming life; and (2) to serve the Lord. You may feel inadequate. Good! You must feel your need before the Lord can help you.

POWER FOR OVERCOMING

The first time you fail, you can expect the devil to tell you, "It's no use. You can't live the Christian life. You might as well give up." This is one of Satan's favorite tactics.

You may even feel defeated because you were tempted— even though you didn't yield. Remember this: *temptation is not sin.* Even Jesus was tempted.

Know Your Weak Points. You have read, or will read, about Peter today. When the apostle learned Jesus would be betrayed, he boldly said he was willing to die for the Lord. But before the night was over he had denied the Lord three times. If you have trouble with temper or some other human weakness, be on guard.

Cooperate with God. Rely on Jesus to help you overcome. A little girl said, "Jesus is stronger than the devil, so when the devil comes to the door of my heart, I send Jesus, and when the devil sees Jesus, he goes away."

Christ lives in your heart through His Holy Spirit, who is

called "the Comforter," meaning "one called alongside to help." He will develop in you the fruit of the Spirit (see Galatians 5:22,23) which together are the character of Christ. (Remember, in chapter 4 I mentioned God's purpose is to make you like Christ.) Try underlining in John 14 and 16 the things which Jesus promised the Holy Spirit would do.

An obedient attitude will help. Obey the Lord when He suggests something to you. Listen to the pastor and other mature Christians. They've been over the road; they can help you.

Cultivate a sense of the Lord's presence. This is part of the abiding Jesus mentions in chapter 15. Let your thoughts go out toward Him throughout the day.

Don't get discouraged. You don't need to give up, and you shouldn't. A baby starting to walk often falls, but it mustn't give up. Simply come to the Lord as you did the first time, ask Him in sincerity to forgive you, and go on.

POWER FOR SERVICE

The Holy Spirit has a work to do for you, after salvation and different from it. It is called the baptism in the Holy Spirit and is the same experience we read about in Acts 2. Before He went away, Jesus told His disciples He would baptize them in the Holy Spirit. As a result they would receive power to witness unto Him. This happened on the Day of Pentecost and changed the lives of all who received. Ask your pastor to tell you more about this.

Jesus Is the Baptizer. How do you receive? The simplest way to put it I can think of is to tell you to get just as close to Jesus as you can. Move toward Him in worship and praise. Then yield completely to Him. Your experience will be just like that on the Day of Pentecost.

16

The Baptism Is a Beginning. Sad to say, some stand still spiritually after they have been baptized in the Holy Spirit. This should not be. It should be the beginning of a wonderful new kind of life. Through you God can work supernaturally.

Stay Spirit-filled. The baptism in the Holy Spirit is not a once-for-all experience. As you continue to stay close to the Lord in prayer and reading His Word, you will receive from Him more and more of His life and blessing.

BIBLE STUDY FOR TODAY

John 13:34,35. What was Jesus' new commandment?

_____

John 14:6. What is the only way to come to God? _____

_____

John 14:13,14. What is the secret of receiving answers to our prayers? _____

John 14:15. How do we show our love for Jesus? _____

_____

John 14:27. What has Jesus promised to give us? _____

_____

John 15:5. Who is the vine, and who are the branches?

_____

John 15:18,19. What attitude can we expect from the world (unbelievers)? _____

_____

GOOD VERSES TO MEMORIZE: John 13:35; 14:6; 14:14; 14:27; 15:5

17

6
What Does God Expect of Me?

TODAY'S BIBLE READING: John 16, 17, and 18

In John 16:7, you will read that the Holy Spirit "will guide you into all truth." Some phases of this truth will be very pleasant, but some phases will emphasize your responsibilities as a child of God.

It's all a part of growing up spiritually, you see. In the natural, a child has a very carefree life. But as he matures, he must assume some responsibilities. You don't want to remain a spiritual baby, of course. Let's see some of the responsibilities which now are yours.

MAKE CHRIST THE MASTER

To express their loyalty to Jesus when He was living on earth, His disciples often called Him "Lord" or "Master." Jesus accepted this position and said, "If ye love me, keep my commandments" (John 14:15).

You see, as a believer, you now belong to Christ. You did belong to Satan, but Christ has bought you with His blood. When we realize how much Jesus has done for us, how He died for us, how He saved us from hell, we are glad for opportunities to show our love for Him by obeying Him.

PUT CHRIST FIRST IN YOUR LIFE

This topic will include anything else I could say to you. Cultivate a sense of Christ's presence. Talk to Him in prayer—at definite times, and also when by yourself throughout the day. When reading the Bible, think of it as Jesus talking to you. Make Jesus the center of your life.

GIVE CHRIST YOUR TIME

There should be a change in your life and habits. If you really want to be a successful Christian, you will want to attend every church service. You will want to have a definite time of private devotions—and of family devotions, if you have a family. You will want to participate in church activities. All this takes time—but it will be worth it!

GIVE CHRIST YOUR ABILITIES

Everyone can do something. If you have special talents, dedicate them to the Lord's work. You may want to take training to develop some latent ability. Besides the jobs which call for special talents, there are many, many other tasks where you can help. Your pastor, or other church leaders, will be delighted to have you volunteer. Here is a suggestion I've found helpful: promise the Lord you will try to do anything you are asked to do.

GIVE CHRIST YOUR MATERIAL POSSESSIONS

I said earlier that you belong to the Lord. That means all you own too. It's not really giving to the Lord, since He owns it already. What we give is an investment in the greatest business in the world—the gospel. You will want to begin tithing—contributing a tenth of your income to the work of God. It looks hard to do? I promise you, you will find the nine-tenths going farther than the whole.

BECOME A MEMBER OF A CHURCH

You belong to a new family—the people of God. Show

19

you belong to the family by joining a Bible-believing church. It will give you an increased sense of belonging and will provide an increased opportunity to help others. Through your church and its ministries, you can reach to the ends of the earth. You will find your church ministering to your own needs too.

TELL OTHERS OF YOUR FAITH

Someone told you about Christ, probably, or you would not be saved today. Don't you think you have an obligation to help others too? As you witness at every opportunity, you will become constantly more effective. Next to your salvation, your greatest thrill will be leading someone else to Christ. Talk to someone every day.

BIBLE STUDY FOR TODAY

John 16:7. Why was it necessary for Jesus to go away?

_____

John 16:13–15. Tell two things the Holy Spirit will do.

_____

_____

John 16:33. What will we have in the world? _____

_____ In Christ? _____

John 17:9. What is Jesus doing for us? _____

_____

John 18:38. What did Pilate say of Jesus? _____

_____

GOOD VERSES TO MEMORIZE: John 16:24; 16:33; 17:3; 17:15

7
How Can I Know the Will of God?

TODAY'S BIBLE READING: John 19, 20, and 21

How to know the will of God—that's a big enough subject to rate a book in itself. And it's important. After all, if Christ is now your Master, and you want to obey Him, you must know what He wants you to do.

WHEN IT'S A MATTER OF CONDUCT

It's obvious the Bible doesn't cover every detail of modern-day living. Matters of everyday activity now were unknown when the Bible was written. But of one thing you can be sure: the Bible contains principles which cover every situation. I'll mention some which you will find helpful. Look for others and make a note of them.

Some Can, Others Cannot. This does not refer to acts of sin, of course. But in matters about which the Bible is silent, remember God deals with people as individuals. Don't expect everyone to fit into your mold.

Consider Others. Some things which you find acceptable might cause another Christian to fail. Paul once said that if acting a certain way would cause another Christian to stumble, he'd be willing never to do it again, even though he saw no wrong in it himself.

Is It Glorifying to God? You are now Jesus' representative in the world. You should do nothing to bring shame or reproach upon your Lord or His cause.

There are many principles, of course, but the most important is to *be guided by your love for Jesus*. Above all else, ask yourself, "Will this be pleasing to the Lord?" If you make that the ruling question in your decisions, you won't go far wrong.

WHEN YOU MUST DECIDE WHICH WAY TO GO

There will be times when you just do not know which course of action to follow. (I'm talking about life decisions now, not matters of conduct.) How can you decide?

Be patient. A Bible verse states, "He that believeth shall not make haste." Learn to wait on God until He indicates His will to you. Time has a way of working things out. Don't be rash. Don't make a move until the path is clear.

Seek the Advice of Others. Don't be a "loner." Let your pastor or some other mature Christian be your confidant. Be sure it is someone who will keep your confidence. Someone who is not involved in the problem can see the various angles of the problem more clearly than you can.

Commit the Matter to the Lord. A famous Christian used this method: He would list the reasons for and against a certain course of action and prayerfully consider the matter for a time. Then he would decide to move in a certain direction. He would remove from his mind as much of his own desires as possible, then ask the Lord to block his path if it were not God's will. Over a period of fifty years he found this approach successful, judging by the way matters turned out.

GETTING ALONG WITH OTHERS

Getting along with others is one of the most important aspects of Christian living.

If you haven't learned this yet, you will soon discover

that Christians are not perfect. As in your case, God is trying to develop their characters, to make them like Jesus.

Some people you will like instinctively; others will not be particularly attractive to you. Just remember this: there are traits in you also which may not be especially attractive to some.

The most important gift you can ask from God is the gift of love—for God and for others. Love includes all the other traits God wants to develop in you. Love will keep you walking close to the Lord. Love for others will make you considerate of them. Love will make you want to win others to the Lord. God can even give you a love for the unlovely.

BIBLE STUDY FOR TODAY

John 19:7,8. Why was Pilate afraid? _____

_____

What phrase, repeated in John 19:24, 28, and 36, shows that Jesus' death was planned? _____

_____

John 20:7. What item did Peter notice particularly in the tomb? _____

John 20:31. Why was the Gospel of John written? _____

_____

John 21:15. What important question did Jesus ask Peter? _____

John 21:22. How did Jesus answer Peter's curiosity? __

_____

GOOD VERSES TO MEMORIZE: John 20:21; 20:31

What Now?

Well, the first seven days are over. How did you do? Now, what about the future? Let me reemphasize some points and give you some more tips.

Bible Reading. Read the Bible every day and all the way through once a year. It will take only 10–15 minutes a day. Read the Gospel of John through two more times at least; then start at Matthew and read through Acts. Now read the story portions of the Old Testament, beginning with Genesis; then read the New Testament all the way through. Finally, begin at Genesis and read through the whole Bible.

Prayer. Prayer is the lifeline of your spiritual life. In your private times, make this a conversation with God. Think of Him as a Great Friend you can confide in. Talk to Him about your victories as well as your needs.

The Baptism in the Holy Spirit. Seek to be filled.

If You Fail. You don't have to fail, understand, but if you do, ask God for forgiveness, just as you did the first time. He will never give up on you. But determine by His help not to fail in the same way again.

Find a Church Home. Become a member of a good church and help in every way possible.

Be Baptized in Water. The Lord has commanded water baptism. It is one of the ways you can give a public testimony to your conversion.

Become a Tither. Give ten cents out of every dollar you earn at the church you have made your church home.

What Now? It depends on you. If you follow these suggestions, you will have the most wonderful, satisfying life possible.